T0103889

Death did not take my dogs....

ANGELS did!!!!

TRINI DEYARMIN

WESTBOW°
PRESS
A DIVISION OF THOMAS NELSON
& ZONDERVAN

Copyright © 2014 Trini Deyarmin.

All rights reserved. No part of this book may be used or reproduced by any means, graphic, electronic, or mechanical, including photocopying, recording, taping or by any information storage retrieval system without the written permission of the publisher except in the case of brief quotations embodied in critical articles and reviews.

WestBow Press books may be ordered through booksellers or by contacting:

WestBow Press
A Division of Thomas Nelson & Zondervan
1663 Liberty Drive
Bloomington, IN 47403
www.westbowpress.com
1 (866) 928-1240

Because of the dynamic nature of the Internet, any web addresses or links contained in this book may have changed since publication and may no longer be valid. The views expressed in this work are solely those of the author and do not necessarily reflect the views of the publisher, and the publisher hereby disclaims any responsibility for them.

Any people depicted in stock imagery provided by Thinkstock are models, and such images are being used for illustrative purposes only. Certain stock imagery © Thinkstock.

ISBN: 978-1-4908-4258-5 (sc)
ISBN: 978-1-4908-4257-8 (e)

Library of Congress Control Number: 2014911520

Printed in the United States of America.

WestBow Press rev. date: 06/30/2014

Contents

In
Memory
Of
Cricket and Copper

Preface

As I've aged, my short and long term memory seems not to be one of my strong points. Losing my second dog, a year after my first one, was extremely emotional. So, to my surprise when all the memories started flooding into my head, I decided to write them down. I definitely did not have a book in mind when I started. My thoughts were of healing, and the best way to heal was to write a memory journal.

It wasn't until two, three-year-old boys made my whole journal come alive. God then overwhelmingly pressed on my heart to write down what happened in order to share with others his precious gifts to us. (Romans 6:23)

Thank you so much to Deena and Gianna who helped put my writings together. A special thank you to my heavenly father who loves me so much to bless Owen and Cooper, just to make my life so much happier!

04.01.2014

05.13.2014

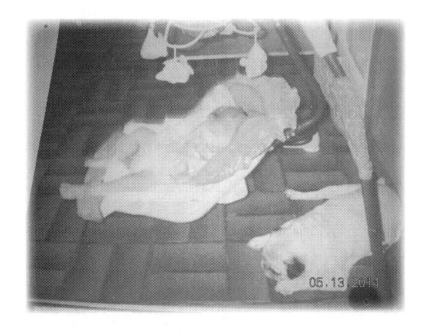

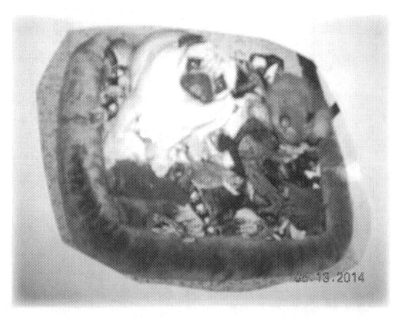

Like a good dog owner that I wanted to be, I read up on some dogs I thought I would like. You know, the ones that are the least maintenance, won't eat you out of house and home, or require daily baths due to running through the mud. I also didn't want to offend my neighbors with a dog that barks day and night or chases their cats into a frenzy. Some people want to buy a dog for their child, who begs and cries to have one, knowing full well that they will be the ones taking care of it. They shouldn't worry though, because that same child will grow up, get married, and buy a precious puppy for their child. Then under their breath, those parents can only hope that their child's dog is a mischievous creature that challenges them every day, due to neglecting their childhood dog in the past. So, for you parents, just pick out what you truly like.

As you're driving around, you might spot the very well-trained dogs sitting in their owner's yards, minding their own business, not barking or disturbing the peace. How exactly did they train that dog to be so good? What we don't realize is that these people were either blessed with the perfect dog, or we missed the poor dog getting zapped to death by the invisible, electric fence! Visions then come to mind of how to have good, obeying, loving kids but are quickly discarded as wrong.

So, my husband, Swanny, and I discussed qualities we really didn't want our dog to have, like the strength to knock down the children who we babysat at our house (later, our small dog proved us wrong!). I didn't want an outside dog that I thought would freeze during our Buffalo winter months, nor did he want a dog like Clifford the Big Red Dog, digging holes and burying bones in our yard. We also didn't want one small enough that we would trip over and hurt. We know better now; dogs don't move when they are comfortable, and you are the only one who gets hurt when you trip on them! Have you ever seen the dog cartoons where the dog is walking the owner instead of the owner walking the dog? Well, we didn't want that either.

With so many breeds to choose from, I didn't know where to start, until one day, when my heart was stolen. I saw a dog owner walking their prim and proper pug. You know, one of the breeds you see on The National Dog Show on TV after the Macy's Thanksgiving Day Parade. Very well-groomed and perfect. When I arrived home, I searched the Internet for information on pugs. I was pleased to read they didn't shed much, were well-behaved with kids, and didn't have many outstanding health issues. My husband and I then found an owner a town away and made an appointment to check out the litter.

Our pug was an only pup litter, which actually was a relief that we didn't have to make the hard choice of picking the cutest amongst the cute. The mommy pug seemed nice enough as we sat on the floor playing with the pup. The mother was fawn in color and appeared a

We had a blanket and bed all ready for her. She looked like a small hamster, and she was so tiny. I realize now that we must have looked like gentle giants in that small puppy's eyes. Gentle giants who were constantly picking her up all the time. Sadly, she occasionally got an accidental kick when we hurried through the kitchen and did not see her bitty little self, which always resulted in many tears and soft hugs.

One of her favorite spots to lay was with her head propped on the bottom of the screen door, looking outside. Now that I think back, I wonder if she was missing her mommy ever so much. I was drawn to her sad face. Would I ever get her to smile? I sure was going to try.

We put up a gate on the kitchen door that leads to the rest of the house. Well that gate, I have to say, turned into quite a death trap for Swanny! I could be in one of my saddest moods, and he would somehow trip going over or through that gate and land smack right on his face! The insults to doggie gates turned out to be very common around our home.

So, like all new puppies, she cried the first night. I sat on the edge of the bed waiting, and, to my surprise, she stopped. The repeating thought to go check on her kept me from sleeping, so I went downstairs and found that she wasn't all cozy in the bed I made for her.

The search began. I looked everywhere for her.

My kitchen was big, but this was ridiculous! Where was my baby pug? I tried calling the name that we had picked for her, but like that was going to work. I'm certain the puppy was thinking, who me? Now, panic-stricken, I went racing upstairs to my husband, who obviously wasn't worried but rather annoyed that I woke him. With alarm and fear I said, "I can't find her! She's gone. Or maybe she is stuck under the stove or dishwasher or hot tub!" Tears streaming down my face.

I hurried back downstairs, Swanny slowly following and, lo and behold, there sat my sweet, baby pug in the middle of the floor with a look of innocence.

That was the beginning of many sleepless nights to check on her. To make myself feel better, I managed to buy four more dog beds and strategically placed them around the kitchen and bathroom, so my baby pug would feel loved and not lost. Now, of course, her favorite spot was not the pretty beds I bought but on top of or in our slippers or shoes that we left by the door. Most parents can relate. Children never like the expensive gifts we buy them, but those old pots and pans are their favorite toys!

It wouldn't be until later that I realized that angels were watching over my pug.

I can't even imagine the job Adam had in the Bible for coming up with all the names for the animals! Naming the pug, however, was a brain teaser as to which family member would be lucky enough to have their preferred name chosen. With much arguing, debating, and losing sleep, I finally came up with the name. Cricket.

If I remember right, wasn't there a phone company named Cricket? My boys, Kyle and Kurtis, naturally said that's a stupid name because dogs don't hop. My argument was that at least the dog will come when she is called. Get it? Called? Later, my boys would argue, "Why does the dog keep getting treats and we don't?" The jury is still out on whether it's harder to train kids or the dog. Then again, I will have to admit, I think the dog and the kids won on the training debate -- none of them are trained! As a mush for a parent, I apparently loved way more than I trained.

Obviously, I had to show off my prized puppy with her new name to the neighbors, who owned a big ol' black lab. What was I thinking, putting a tiny puppy the size of a softball next to such a big dog? They sniffed each other out upon meeting, then Cricket ran circles around the monster of a dog. So, instinctively the black lab assumed she wanted to play and started rolling her around like a soccer ball! Of course, my baby pug rolled easily enough, but I was horrified, swooping in like a hawk to pick her up, securely holding her in my arms from the big brute. The dogs probably could have been best friends, but my motherly instinct was to keep her away from rough playing neighbors!

The name Cricket got used a lot as we chased her outside, begging her not to go to the neighbors! Her nickname ended up being Cric-Cric, which was fitting for her when she got older and her bones were hurting. I'm sure if dogs could talk, she would have asked me why I named her the name of an insect, but I would assure her that I was thinking of the Cricket phone company.

Ask me or my dog if we like winter, and we will both tell you no, so potty training in the snow was not happening. I opted for training the puppy on newspapers. Every accident the puppy had, we would tell her, "No, no!" and set her back on the papers and tell her, "Yes, yes!" We would explain to her that we didn't care if she peed on certain articles in the paper, like our taxes going up again, but we did care if her pee landed on the kitchen floor. At one point, I thought she might be blind due to the fact that she kept missing the papers. Of course, she decided it was funny to drag all the papers around the kitchen and still miss! So feeling defeated, I covered the entire kitchen floor with newspapers, and, to my surprise, BINGO she peed on the papers. Every day I made her newspaper area smaller and smaller until it led to a corner with a doggie tray and absorbent pads. We were both finally happy.

So you may ask why I stuck with indoor training like a cat. My theory was based on the fact that I watched children all day, and if I didn't locate the poop outside before the children did, well, I think you know where I'm going with this.

Now there was one thing that there is just no training for -- hairballs and diarrhea. We never knew when or where she was going to hack up something or occasionally have diarrhea in some unexpected place in our house.

As she got older, we did attempt to set her in the grass a few times without a leash to play, but her only thoughts were -- escape! Off to the neighbor's house she went, at least 200 feet away. She would occasionally look back and laugh as we wearily chased after her. Ever try catching a bunny rabbit? Well, a pug is that fast. She would have me running back in the house to fetch her favorite treat that I would attempt to bribe her with. I swear she had eyes in the back of her head because as my husband snuck up behind her, and I had the treat in front of her, she hopped around not letting us catch her (and the kids said she didn't hop...).

To my pleasure, early on training her, I decided not to teach her to go down steps, only up. This was so she would stay on the deck and porch with no way down to visit the neighbors unexpectedly. Also, we had lots of hawks in the area in the summer, and we didn't want them to think my pug truly was a bunny rabbit they could eat.

It's a known fact that dogs have a keen sense of hearing, and Cricket was no exception. She could hear the mail lady's brakes across the street at my mailbox when she delivered the mail everyday. Never did I think that one sunny day Cricket would take off out my sliding glass doors attached to the deck, 90 miles per hour, as only pugs can do, slide right through the deck railing, land on all fours, and chase the mail truck! After a much needed scolding, I added more spindles to my railing.

She never did take a liking to that leash. She would kindly let me put it on her, but once outside, she would do her best to try to wiggle out of it. We even gave her the benefit of the doubt one day and took her without a leash; not one of our smarter ideas. We had a path mowed about 900 feet long in a corn field where the tractors parked that we traveled for walks. Now, you would think Cricket could stay on the nice, mowed path and behave -- not! About 100 feet in, off she darted through the corn field, bringing me to instant tears and the thought that we would never find her. After calling her and calling her, she finally found her way back as I yelled, "I got treats!"

Like I said, we never had to train that good hearing of Cricket's. We dared not get up in the middle of the night to have to go pee, due to squeaky floorboards. That meant that we were up, and Cricket was ready to meet us at the bottom of the stairs. If we tried sneaking back to bed, she would cry and whine, making us feel badly enough until someone came down to see her. Ironically, that same dog during the day would flip on her back and snore something awful, and it didn't matter how noisy the house was with all the kids playing and televisions on. Cricket also used her good hearing for neighbors when their car doors shut. She would alarm us with barking when they left or came back. Ironically, the only time she decided not to alarm us was when someone actually broke into our truck one night!

We apparently annoyed her when we plugged and unplugged our computer, which sounded like a doorbell and would send her into a barking frenzy.

You would have thought I bought a hound dog, trained to find birds. Cricket would wake up from a coma sleep if a bird tweeted on the television or outside. There was no way to hit the mute button fast enough to stop her from barking for five whole minutes! So, that meant my deck and porch were off limits to the birds; so much for my friendly bird feeders.

One humorous bird had actually managed to build her nest in the gutter near our deck, or should I say, Cricket's deck. When Cricket discovered what happened, she sat guard on the deck for days, staring at that mommy bird, not letting her out of her sight. Put it this way, if her eyes could have killed it, that bird would have been a goner! I'm sure that mommy bird explained to her babies that this was a bad nesting area, due to attack dogs. She never nested there again much to Cricket's relief, but just in case, though, every time a bird came close to the deck or railings, she would mark the territory with pee. Of course later, when I got a second puppy, she thought it would be a cool thing to do by being a copycat. It made quite the assault on my stained deck boards, but I did laugh how hard she tried to be a good watch dog.

Where is the camera when you need it? While Cricket was on deck duty, she managed to fall into one of those coma sleeps while lying in the sun. This very bold squirrel with a nut in her claws decided to get within an inch of her. Only the Lord knows what she was thinking, and I swear that squirrel must have said, "Boo!" because Cricket jumped up on all fours, frightening that poor squirrel so badly he threw his nut in the air and ran!

Once again, I researched on the Internet which dog food would be the best for my precious puppy. To my surprise, regular dog food included a lot of ingredients that either I didn't know what they were, or I didn't want my puppy eating them, so I went the all natural route and did a lot of my own cooking. What I came up with was rice, vegetables, and turkey. Yum. Sounds like a good meal. We also had to decide whether to feed them twice or three times a day. We decided on three times, but later when she got older, we switched it to twice a day. For the next 11 years, my pug ate that recipe of food, and her weight stayed consistent and she was healthy. Unlike Swanny and I, who gained a few pounds as we aged. However, Cricket did not like peas in her food. To my amazement, she would gulp down her food in record time, and I'm not exaggerating when I say gulped, and leave all the peas at the bottom of the bowl! That's talent! It's sort of like us trying to do that with Lucky Charms and leaving all the marshmallows for last. I eventually started leaving out the peas.

The most adorable and amazing thing was watching our pug puppy eat for the first time and her back feet rising up in the air! Well, that sent me flying to the pet store to get a dish her height so she could eat on all fours.

Now feeding a pug medications, well, that was a whole different story. I think Cricket knew it was all trickery. As I tried to disguise that stupid pill in everything from pizza to meatballs, she could still smell it! The only way I could trick her was to give her three or four treats without the pill, and as she was gulping them down, quickly slip in the medicated one. What. A. Chore.

On a normal day, though, giving her a treat was a task in general. I think her bulgy eyes made the treats look very big. Due to that impression, she would always nip my fingers, even if I told her to bite gently. So, I resorted to tossing the treats, so she could catch them in her mouth. She ended up being a pro at that. Of course, I forgot to tell a few people about this, as they got their fingers nipped, like the mailman one day trying to give her a treat. Later, my next dog would think tossing them was a stupid game and would make me gingerly give her the treat instead.

I will say, Cricket was smart by sitting under the kids' chairs during meals and devouring all the dropped food; so much for that three second rule. Sometimes, though, eating too many snacks or scraps would cause belly aches, which, in turn, would cause throwing it back up. I'm sure any normal household would have a few minutes to clean it up, but I always had to be quick about it, before one of the many people in my house stepped in it.

I decided to surprise Cricket one day with barbecue rib bones, which later both dogs enjoyed chewing on. One day, when I ran out of them, I went to the store to fetch some more. Unfortunately, they ran out of the barbecue flavored ones so I bought regular instead. You know, it's bad enough when your own kids give you a hard time about groceries, but the dogs too? They absolutely refused to touch those bones because they had no barbecue sauce. Next time, I bought the good ones in bulk.

First of all, Cricket loved the babies I watched. She would sleep under their swing, and when the babies were in a stroller, she would stay as close to them as she could, without getting run over. She was also my shadow wherever I went -- always in the same room or the nearest she could get to me. If I was in the bathroom, she would sit in front of the bathroom door and wait. If I was upstairs, she would wait at the bottom of the stairs. When I went outside, she would sit on the deck or porch, wherever would make her closest to me in the yard. If I sat on the couch, though, she was either at my feet or the opposite end of the couch, definitely not a cuddlier.

Sunbathing was her favorite thing to do. Every time the sun was out, she would sit at the sliding glass door and whine until I opened it. Once outside, she would pick the sunniest spot, roll on her back and put all fours in the air, tanning her belly. I have to tell you that living in NY the sun is very deceiving. You look out the window, see the sun shining, grab your sneakers, and run outside, only to run back in to grab a sweatshirt. Now, I swear that pug either had memory loss or loved to annoy me, because every ten minutes, she would whine to go out and see if the sun was warmer yet because she didn't like the cold.

After a while, my husband and I finally got smart and invested in one of those doggie doors. We didn't want one of the permanent ones for security reasons, so we invested in one that we could install and uninstall easily from the sliding glass doors. For some reason, Cricket did not want me to have one up on her, so she refused to use it! You pug owners know that pugs love treats or food in general, so after all attempts of sticking my head, my feet, and my hands through the doggie door to prove to her it was safe, I had to resort to treats. I know Cricket thought I wasn't playing fair, but I always thought she wasn't willing to negotiate. Once showing her the delicious treat I had, I would sit it outside the doggie door. Cricket was worse than a small child with making me feel badly. She would sit and stare at it through the glass doors and cry. After many stabs at it, I was finally able to coax her through the door while holding it open. You would think the story ended there, but then Cricket would wonder how I could be so mean to leave her outside, and the only way back in was through that dumb doggie door. Needless to say, it took two weeks before she felt totally safe to use it and a few pounds heavier from all the treats.

Living in the country would always bring about a few stray cats. Now I wouldn't say I hate cats, but only that I owned a devil of one and finally had to give it away. Therefore, cats who taunt Cricket, I'm not really fond of, or the ones who spray on my porch. Those darn cats would prance around my garden, until they caught the attention of Cricket in the window and send her into a barking frenzy. Then, they would continue to harass her because she could not touch them. Well, this would get me up from any quiet moment I was having and go outside and scare them off till another day. Afterward, as I was calming Cricket down, she would look up at me with her big eyes and say, "Good job. That cat didn't have a chance!"

After a while, she was very proud to use the doggie door, but it only led to the deck, so if I was in the front yard, she couldn't see me. So Swanny and I decided to build a bridge between the deck and porch which proved to be a good idea. It didn't take much encouraging to get Cricket to go over the bridge, and she seemed pleased with it. Little did we think about the poor mail lady.

So one day, as Cricket sat on the back of the couch, watching for cats and guarding our house, the mail lady decided to deliver a package to my door. Cricket flew off my couch, quick as a lightning bolt. I don't even think her paws hit the floor, and she sailed through the living room, dining room, kitchen, out the doggie door, over the bridge, to the porch, to scare the poor mail lady to death! I thank God every day I never taught that pug to go down those steps. Naturally, I started getting Post-It notes that said my packages were at the post office.

Sometime later, I realized that if I wanted to shut the screen only on my sliding glass doors, Cricket would not have her doggie door. To my surprise, they make a doggie screen door. What I didn't anticipate was a 17 pound pug racing through it in a hurry, ripping it right out! I spent more time fixing it than she did using it. I suppose that some dog owners have scratched up doors; I had the ripped out screens.

When people called ahead of time to see if they could stop over, I would lock the doggie door so Cricket wouldn't alarm my visiting friends. Now, due to her occasional short memory span, she would come barreling around the corner, and, yup, smack right into the locked doggie door and flatten her little pug face a little more!

Later, my other puppy would use that doggie door to her advantage, or, should I say, annoyance. She would go through it and sit and block the door so Cricket could not get out. Left poor Cricket whining on what to do.

CHAPTER 8

Other Memories

I don't know if it was due to her being short, but one of Cricket's favorite spots to sit was on the back of the couch like a cat, looking out the window. Unfortunately, due to dog allergies, she would sneeze on my windows, making it an awful mess. Like I mentioned before, nobody could come near the house without her noticing. She loved to greet people with a friendly wagging of the tail and get her head petted. Everyone would be convinced how friendly she was until they tried to leave. For some unknown pug reason, she turned into an attack dog when visitors tried to depart. She would start barking and growling at them and attacking pant legs, trying to stop them from leaving.

If she ever got scolded for a mishap, then she would hide behind the bathroom door and watch through the crack to see where we were.

We loved watching movies when they had a pug in them. It made us feel proud our breed of dog was a star. Who knows, maybe they were even a distant relative!

Talk about spoiling her, though, we decided one day to invest in a very fancy doghouse so Cricket could be outside with the kids and us, of course, on a chain. As usual, she absolutely refused to go near the doghouse, whatever she thought it was. So, there it sits. However, I did get creative one day and purchased a stone life-like dog that sits next to the dog house very happily.

Swanny and I would like to go to different places to eat or visit, which left Cricket at home by herself. We would always try to remember to bring a treat home with us, so that Cricket knew we were missing her as well. After a while, I would feel guilty about leaving her, so we decided to buy her a friend.

CHAPTER 9

Bringing Home a Friend

As many of us dog owners do when we see other puppies other than our own, we say, "Aww, how cute they are! Let's get another one." I felt remorseful that Cricket didn't have a dog friend. Cricket proved to us she definitely wasn't the cuddly type, which should have rung a bell in my head as to her not wanting a friend around. So, instead of just getting any ol' dog, we thought, well, let's breed her, make a few bucks, and keep one of the babies. Lots of people do that. We made a couple phone calls and ended up contacting a breeder not too far away and set up an appointment.

Not in a million years, Cricket was apparently thinking. I've got to tell you, we tried twice and not only would she not enjoy the company of other playful pugs, but she growled at them and wouldn't let anyone sniff or touch her! Okay, so enough with that idea.

Instead we went in search of the cuddly dog we always wanted, not really sure what breed to get. Then one day Swanny just showed up with this adorable fluff ball of a Pomeranian. Now this one did not have kennel papers, but I instantly fell in love. She looked like the dogs that Hollywood celebrities would carry around in their purses. I was convinced this was a great idea, so that Cricket would have a friend and be thrilled -- not!

If looks could kill, I would have been dead. How dare I bring such a creature to her home. That baby Pom immediately jumped into Cricket's bed and made herself cozy! Cricket went right under the kitchen table and pouted. The Pom tried to snuggle with her, play with her, love her but to no avail. It took four weeks for Cricket to get over being mad at me or to even look at that puppy. All of us moms can relate to bringing home a new baby brother or sister, and them not getting a welcome party from their siblings.

Undoubtedly, our Pom was relentless every day, trying to be Cricket's best friend. Of course, it was funny when Cricket refused to play and would just lie there. The puppy would jump on her back and try to wrestle with her. Once again, where was my camera when she would jump on Cricket's head and sit there a moment, like she was deep in thought, only to make Cricket look like she had a whole new hairdo!

Now, back to that name game again. A few pretty names came to mind like Pebbles or Princess, but then we decided to keep it to a "C" name to match Cricket's. There were only a thousand of them to choose from.

Since we watched kids a lot, that meant that we saw quite a few Disney movies. Our new puppy reminded us of *The Fox and The Hound* and presto! We had her name. Copper.

Copper ended up being our love bug, but Cricket was going to have no part of that, and she was adamant we didn't either. When you bring home a new baby, it's just instinct to want to pick her up all the time to hold her. So Cricket who was one and a half, decided she suddenly wanted to be picked up, too. Hoping to appease her, I would pick her up, but she wiggled to get back down after 10 seconds. Little did I know, her only goal was getting me to put down Copper. Who ever said dogs were dumb? If I tried to pick up Copper again, Cricket would go into a barking fit. So, if my husband or I wanted to pick up Copper, we had to wait until Cricket was asleep, sneak Copper out of the room, and hold her. That would last until Cricket would wake up and catch us red-handed!

Some mornings, not very many, we would quietly come downstairs and catch the puppies sleeping together and take a picture to prove it. Actually, what I think happened is Cricket was too tired to move when Copper jumped in bed with her. I would smile and Cricket would look at me with this disgusted look since she was our first baby.

In the evenings when we sat and watched television, Copper would be on our laps. But good ol' Cricket, who hated to play or be bothered, would go out to the kitchen and bring in the toys and look like she wanted to play. Now Copper, who was young and naïve, would jump right off our laps to go play. Cricket would start to play, and then go back to bed.

Copper had such high hopes of Cricket being her friend that she continued to try every day; she was such a love bug. Honestly, I think Copper sort of grew on her like one of those annoying friends we sometimes acquire in life. Just to prove how dedicated Copper was, she would clean Cricket's eyes and ears out every morning. It was funny to watch Cricket try to avoid her. Later in their lives, Cricket got an ulcerated eye and the first thing the vet said was don't let the other dog lick her in the eye. Yeah right. That's like telling a coffee drinker, let's not have coffee this morning! You'll get through it! My first thought was to tape Copper's mouth shut, but a good dog owner puts that ridiculous cone on Crickets head. That only caused her to do flips in her bed trying to get the darn thing off. Since the cone was doing more damage than good, I removed it and resorted to scare Copper with, "No!" every time her tongue remotely came out of her mouth, then I would pick her up and love her because I felt sorry.

Copper would let Cricket be in control for the most part, allowing her to bark when someone arrived or when some action was going on in the house. Of course, the doorbell would put Cricket into an immediate barking rage, and Copper would just sit and watch. Funnier yet, was my husband or I making a mad dash, leaping over toys and furniture to try to answer the door before the doorbell rang and saving Cricket the meltdown of barking. As long as we didn't trip, it made us feel young again for a moment, and both dogs were seemingly amused by the action.

Cricket strived to be my shadow and Copper strived to be Cricket's shadow, so potty training for Copper was easy, well, almost. As soon as Cricket peed, Copper would pee right on top of it, every time. Now, if only our own kids could have been that easy! There was one slight glitch to this buddy system -- Copper couldn't poop on demand. So when Cricket did her business, Copper would jump on the papers, snatch the poop, and run off with it in her mouth! You know that grossed me out to no end, and I would pick up my precious little fluff ball and look into her beautiful brown eyes and say, "No kisses from you for at least two days." So I wish I could say the pooping was just as easy for her, but my Pom's little legs were so short -- yes, I'm making excuses for her -- so she never quite made it to the papers in time, making a mess for us to wake up to every morning. So what does a good dog owner do? The only thing she could think of, cry to her husband! He assured me he could return her and get our money back, but my response was always, "No, you're not returning my little fluff ball!" What's a girl to do? Wipe away the tears and clean up the mess.

Speaking of those short legs, Cricket had already learned to jump up on the couch and used that skill to get away from Copper, I'm sure. She would sit there and snicker as Copper attempted to jump up, resulting in only smashing into the side of the couch. Of course, I'm sure there was much disappointment when we would give Copper a lift up. Eventually, Copper grew long enough legs, and they would both sit butt-to-butt on the back of the couch, proud as peacocks, or, should I say, cat watchers.

Copper did prove to be smart by prancing right through that doggie gate, making Cricket look dumb. Although, Copper ended up being scared of the bridge, go figure. Copper had her own little tricks of bringing twigs from the deck into the house and chewing them into little pieces, making quite the mess. The funniest thing, though, was when they tried to tug their stuffed dog through the doggie door, getting it stuck half way, just like Winnie the Pooh; neither dog could budge it!

Going to the vet's is like taking your vehicle to the repair shop or going grocery shopping. No matter how hard you try, you're not getting out of there without spending a pretty penny!

Ironically, the one and only time my pug would show any affection was at the vet's office. She would attempt to sit on my lap while driving there, I'm sure to help me miss my turn. Once at the vet's office, she would cuddle on my lap in hopes that I would change my mind and take her home. Her first big procedure was clipping her nails and cleaning her teeth, with the removal of a few, as well. Ever try to hold a greased pig? Well, that's what it's like to try to clip a pug's nails. The vet was good; only made her bleed once. So, Cricket never ended up being thrilled about the truck rides. Her opinion was, leave me alone; I'm fine, just like the personality of some people we know.

Teeth brushing was a beast in itself. It just wasn't going to happen with Cricket. She would growl in disapproval. Copper, she apparently loved the taste of the doggie toothpaste. Hair brushing was also a task. Twice a year both of them shed profusely. Can't say whether Cricket enjoyed her brushing, or if she was just trying to annoy me. She would literally spin in circles so fast that I couldn't keep the brush on her. I would just end up brushing her with my hands as she spun. By the way, the information on the Internet that said pugs only shed a little -- they were wrong.

Bath time was fun and a challenge. You know that noise metal shower rings make when you open the shower curtain, sort of a swooshing, squeaking scrape? I've got to tell you, it didn't matter where Copper was, she would always come running when she heard that sound. She loved her baths! The times she realized the noise was only for me or Swanny to get in the shower, she would be mad. She would sit there all pretty with a devious smile on her face, wait until we got in the shower, and then take off with our foot towel every time. The only way our foot towel would be safe is if she got a bath.

Copper would get all scrubbed up looking like a drowned rat and would be disappointed to get out of the water. We would brush her out and blow dry her until she was all pretty again. If I could end the story there I would. As soon as we got her all perfect, she would parade through that doggie door onto the deck, find the nearest bird poop, and, to my horror, ROLL IN IT! Then she would come prancing back in the house like a little innocent child with chocolate on his face. Of course, I was mortified every time she did this, which, unfortunately, was a lot. I was beginning to think she enjoyed the look on my face.

One day she surprised me and didn't roll in the bird poop; she decided to wait until we took a walk in the driveway. I was walking when, suddenly, she snuck off to my garden to roll in the mulch. I think she got pleasure out of the look of disgust on my face, but I laughed due to her looking so ridiculous. That girl would do anything to try to get a second bath. If I gave Copper a dog bone, she would roll on that too! At least she didn't eat the flies she swatted on the windows.

I always found it amusing when I brushed Copper during shedding season. I would actually comb enough off that it looked like I had two Pomeranians. Cricket would wait at my feet until I was done brushing her, and when I put her back down on the floor, she would tackle her. I'm sure it was to say, "Knock it off with all your pretty stuff!" Copper didn't shed too terribly since she shed fur balls for the most part, which were easy to pick up. Cricket, on the other hand, shed so much, we didn't dare wear black clothes in the house or we were a mess!

Now, a bath for Cricket, well, that was an obstacle. As soon as I opened the cabinet door to get the dog shampoo, Cricket was gone. She would duck under the lowest chair in the house and hide, and if I lifted up the chair, then under another she went. Drying her wasn't too difficult as she spun in circles while I dried her with a hair dryer. Never did figure out if she was spinning to unwind or wind up.

Nail clipping for Copper wasn't as taxing as it was for Cricket, because she had beautiful long hair that hid the nails, making it difficult to see them. I eventually figured out how to wrap her up in her bath towel while she was still wet and easily snip the nails, unlike Cricket, who made me pay the vet to clip hers. I think it was a plot to get even for bringing home the Pomeranian in the first place.

Mind you, I never did do any research on the Pomeranian. My husband just decided to surprise me one day, with the cutest, most adorable puppy he could find. Around the time of Copper's third birthday, she started having awful breath, like human morning breath that says don't kiss me yet, I need to brush. So the vet checked her and saw she had a couple bad teeth. With this being her first surgery, I felt nauseous. Luckily, the vet was only five minutes away. They took her in at about 8 AM, and they called me about four hours later, saying she was all done and could go home. When I arrived, they informed me that they had to pull 14 teeth! Once again, there came my horrified look that apparently only Copper could make me do. I had myself a gummy dog -- all gums and hardly any teeth! It didn't affect her smile, though, and her tail wagged enough to make up for it. Well, not at first. She had to growl to show her disapproval as I picked her up. Unfortunately, her couple of teeth left surely didn't stop her from chewing up twigs in the house or eating her bones or playing tug of war with her toys.

Copper for some reason developed an allergy to grass. Usually, during the months of April and September she would get this horrible cough. It would take us days to get it calmed down with allergy pills, so it caused many sleepless nights. It never did stop her from running in the driveway though, with the children, coughing the entire time.

Then those darn fleas! The dogs would, out of nowhere, be itching up a storm. I would buy the more expensive flea pills at the vet's, which seemed to work the best. Later, however, I did some research on that and some of the chemicals can make a lot of dogs sick, so I suggest any dog owner to beware.

You would have thought we had two babies on our hands when it came to thunder storms. Didn't matter what time of the night it was, they would cry at the bottom of the gate until one of us came downstairs to lie with them, on the couch, of course. Now, remember my pug doesn't cuddle, but during a storm, she can't get close enough. It always made for a long night, since the couch was not very comfy.

We went shopping one day and a storm started brewing before we got home. Cricket greeted us anxiously at the door, but Copper was nowhere to be found. We searched all of the downstairs and still no Copper. I finally heard a cry upstairs, which was strange because the stair gate was locked. Sure enough, my dog, who was only seven pounds full grown and had more hair than body, acted like a mouse and squeezed through the gate railings.

Swanny and I must have been exhausted one night when another storm was happening. To our surprise, a furry creature jumped onto our really tall bed, scaring us half out of our minds. Poor Cricket, who weighed 17 pounds, was left at the bottom of the stairs, crying because she couldn't squeeze through the gate. After that, Copper thought it was pretty cool to do that every night, which once again sent me flying to the store to purchase a new gate she couldn't fit through.

Not only did storms bother the dogs, the Fourth of July was not a joyous occasion either, as we had many neighbors who enjoyed lighting fireworks until the wee hours of the night.

CHAPTER 13

Sunshine and Other Antics

Earlier on, I had said how Cricket enjoyed the sunshine. I would be outside for awhile in my garden and Cricket would be sunbathing on the deck. I would occasionally come indoors to check on Copper, thinking that by now she would come when I called her. Nope, not Copper, she would make us search for her. Copper hated hot days and would try to find the coolest spot in the house to hide. Again, she liked seeing me frustrated. Her favorite spot was behind open doors in the corner, preferably on some shoes or under the curtains. One day, I searched and searched relentlessly, and I know she was smirking as I called her name. It was another one of those times she made herself as small as a mouse and crawled under the recliner.

Now if Copper wanted to be mad at us or had one of her doggie teenage mood swings, she would sit backwards a little ways away from us and refuse to look our way, even if we called her. We would have to get out of our chair and go pick her up.

Due to Cricket's plans to escape when we were taking walks outside, I would have to put her on a leash. Now to be fair, I would put a leash on Copper as well. So one day, Copper decided to be funny when an old man showed up to my garage sale. She ran circles around the man and totally wrapped his legs together! I thought the poor man was going to fall! After many apologies, back in the house Copper went.

Though Cricket never wanted to be held, she refused to let Copper get much affection from us either. When we weren't trying to sneak Copper in the other room to pet her, we would occasionally try to sneak her out of the house. But we'd be darned if Cricket wasn't waiting for us when we came back in. She would sneer and growl barking rebukes at Copper for going outside with us.

Since I watched kids during the day, the dogs were kept in the kitchen until the kids left, and then they were free to roam the house downstairs. Cricket was not too fond of the school-aged kids for some reason but loved the babies. Anytime we had a baby in the swing, Cricket would sleep right underneath him or her, as though, she was keeping the baby safe. If the baby was in the stroller or high-chair, Cricket was always nearby. Copper, on the other hand, was horribly jealous of the babies. It was bad enough when the baby lost its pacifier all on its own, but when Copper stole the pacifier from the baby, it was a task everyday to find it. I even tried buying Copper her own, but, of course, that was no fun for her.

Then there was feeding time. What was it about opening a baby food jar that would send Copper into a fit? Maybe from dropping some on the floor one day, she got a taste of that sweet stuff and definitely wanted more. So, needless to say, everyday was a challenge to feed the baby and try to keep Copper quiet. It could have been just plain jealousy because whenever we held the baby, Copper would keep bouncing off our legs, almost knocking us over, until we picked her up. Now, that could have been a scheme to get the baby's pacifier, who knows.

As Cricket got older, she tolerated us holding Copper a hair more, but we always put effort into petting her more, so she knew we loved her.

When we would take Cricket for vet checks, they would say how grey she was getting in the face. I suppose she was, but she was still the same ol' Cricket to me. I would occasionally drag out photos of her and would be quickly reminded of how young she was not too long ago.

If I were to describe Cricket, I would have to say she was a faithful, quiet friend -- not much for arguing and always reliable. Even though she appeared mad at me when I brought Copper home for the first time, I think as the years rolled on by, she might have thought she didn't really need or want a friend, but was thankful to me for thinking of her.

If dogs could talk, I'm sure she would have pointed out to me all the things that Copper did to annoy her. It reminds me so much of human relationships and the different personalities our friends have.

I wish she would have been cuddlier, but 17 pounds might have been too much for me to carry after lugging around kids all day. Copper, though, made up for it and then some. Thinking back now, that was probably one of the reasons I liked pugs so much; their sad faces made me want to pick them up and make them happy. That's probably why I work so well with kids; I enjoy making them happy.

I felt sad when Cricket couldn't jump on the couch any more. I started giving her omega 3 oils in her food, which did help limber her up some. If I were a cartoonist, I would want to draw dogs walking with canes, telling jokes about their aching old bodies. I would like to tell you she got better about the nail clippings, but old habits die hard.

It's sadly ironic that we come into this world as babies. We can't talk but can only cry when something is wrong. When you watch a dog age, it's much the same; you see they have something wrong but you don't know how to help.

People say that a dog's age is its years multiplied by seven, so Cricket would have been 77 years old. When I look back, it's scary how fast her life went. She was born, she lived, and she died. I'm glad human years don't go by quite that fast, but after age 40, I will say, it seems to be going a little quicker downhill.

I do know, in my older years, I enjoy crawling into a nice, warm bed. Notice, I said crawling, not jumping; therefore, I bought an electric blanket to meet my needs. What a great idea to have one invented for dogs, too! So to my delight, I bought one for Cricket. If it didn't make her feel better, it did me. I would laugh when Copper still jumped in bed with her, making her share the new found warmth.

Cricket was not as quick to be my shadow in her later years. She would wait several minutes to see if I came back into the room, before she would move, due to her being too tired to move twice in five minutes. Taking care of kids, I really never stayed put for too long, unless it was officially nap time. The noise from the kids never bothered her much, but I'm sure she enjoyed the weekends as much as I did.

Cricket still enjoyed lying in the sun but took longer naps. However, she would suddenly spark into lightning bolt speed if the mail lady stopped by to try to deliver a package.

In September, she got a lump on her side and I was concerned it might be cancer. The vet said it was normal but we could have it removed if we wanted. In older pugs, the skin around their mouths gets saggy and the vet was concerned about her chewing on it. So I decided to have them remove the skin on her mouth and watch the lump if it grew. Copper waited all day in the window for Cricket to return. I thought that was so sweet.

Her surgery went well and she was happy to be home. Now the fun part -- she still had to have antibiotics. Let the games begin how I could trick her with treats.

Four months later, the lump decided to grow, so I thought I better have it removed. Again, the surgery went well, but then four days later, her eye ulcerated, and she needed emergency surgery. The surgery was successful, but the first four days to a week I was required to give her eye drops, every four hours to receive the best results. Did I say yet, old age stinks? If all that wasn't bad enough, she started peeing on the floors. The vet assumed it was hormones and put her on hormone pills -- wonderful -- more pills. Later, a nice person at the vet's office finally told me that I could crush up the pills, add water, and put it in an eye dropper. This tip could have saved me ten years of grief, but I suppose that would have been no fun.

She didn't get any better after some time, so back to the vet's we went. He came up with a diagnosis of pyometra, a bacterial infection of the uterus. We started heavy antibiotics, but within days, she woke up in a pile of pus.

It was time to put her down.

I never had my puppies spayed; just didn't want them to go under the knife, if they didn't need to. I am pretty sure now that I shortened their life from lack of knowledge.

First, Swanny and I had to decide who was taking her to be put asleep. I got elected. Our agreement was that I would take Cricket, and he would take Copper when it was time. Second, was the argument of cremation or burial; my husband won on that, many tears later. I was just concerned that if she was buried, something would dig her up and drag her away. I strongly urge any pet owner to have this discussion beforehand; it will save a lot of tears and heartache. Another discussion I would have ahead of time is how much to spend on a sick or dying pet before your spouse divorces you for spending too much.

Neither of us anticipated what was going to happen next. We suddenly had a mourning pet on our hands -- Copper.

CHAPTER 15

Copper's Personality

I never came home with Cricket from the last vet's visit, per se, except in a burial bag. So Copper sat in the window and waited. Every time I came home from an errand, she would check to see if I had Cricket with me. If she didn't see Cricket, back on the couch she went to watch and wait. It was heart wrenching. Copper refused to eat, refused to wag her tail, and refused to play. I didn't know what to do. Those middle-of-the-night eye drops for Cricket were easy compared to cheering up a mourning dog. So, we started by taking her for rides in our truck when we ran errands, which also made us carry lint rollers in the truck, so our seats were not always covered with puff balls from Copper. She started looking forward to that everyday, even if it was a short ride. At first, I think she thought she would be going where she could see Cricket but that never happened. Remembering these rides brings me back to one day when I had to slam on my brakes. My precious seven pound Pomeranian went flying under the dash! I was so alarmed, I pulled right over, lifted her up, and gave her many kisses!

A funnier story yet was when my husband decided to stop over at a friend's house and took Copper with him. He arrived at the house and was chatting with his friend in the driveway but left the truck running. Well, Copper apparently thought he was taking too long and started jumping on the door when my husband heard click click. Yup, she locked him out of his truck! Served him right for taking too long. He had to talk to her excitedly so she wouldn't hide, and he made her keep jumping on the door until it unlocked. He never left the truck again without the keys!

We made several attempts to find her a new companion. We took her to my sister-in-law's house, who had three cats. Copper was so excited, she did her best to try and make friends with the one cat, but the cat only swatted her in the face. When I had garage sales, we would introduce her to any dogs that came, but still they would only growl at her excitement.

She was enthusiastic about the truck rides but not much else. Her sadness sent me running to the store, looking for anything that might cheer her up. I desperately found a motion-activated dog that chased its tail, barked, whined and had big, bulging eyes like Cricket's. When I brought the toy home, at first I think Copper thought it was a real dog, so she was excited. When she quickly discovered it wasn't alive, she decided to ignore it.

We had to hand feed her little bites of food because she refused to eat without Cricket. It was a tradition that they ate together, and if Copper left any in her bowl, Cricket would finish it for her. Copper definitely wouldn't eat the rice mixture I had been feeding her for ten years.

We were running out of ideas, so we took her with us through the McDonalds drive-thru. She wagged her tail a little because she was happy both Swanny and I were in the truck. We got a Big Mac and some chicken nuggets and shared it with her. We had never seen a dog so excited over McDonald's food; she could have been in a commercial for them. The dog does flips over Big Macs. So after three weeks of trying various foods with her, she settled for me cooking her chicken and getting Big Macs at least once a week.

She finally made friends with the motion-activated dog and started to even sleep with it. The only problem was that if she moved in her bed, the dog barked, so she would stay as still as a mouse to keep the dog quiet. Once again I felt a little sorry for her, so I went and bought her a new toy we called Squeakers that would only squeak when she bit it, making her bedtime a little more comfortable. Originally, right after Cricket's death, Copper refused to sleep in any of the beds and would only sleep on the floor. Off to the store for new beds, which she finally did sleep in.

Now, apparently Copper had that same keen sense of hearing like Cricket's or Cricket left her hers. If either my husband or I touched our keys and tried to leave without her, she was right on our heels begging to go. If that didn't work, she would zoom out the door like the Road Runner when we barely even had the door open, and we would look down on the porch, and there she was. We would laugh, pick her up, and set her back in the house. Once I tried to be faster than she was, only to squish her in the door. Yup, that brought instant tears to my eyes and kisses to her. We always tried to make her feel less lonely by keeping the television on in the living room, cartoons, of course, and the radio on in the kitchen.

We took down our death trap gate in the kitchen, which my husband was extremely pleased about, so Copper could play with the kids. She would steal their toys all the time and leave the kids yelling to have them back. One of the kids tried to be sneaky and take Copper's toys. Well, that night, Copper took her toys and hid them. I noticed them missing the next morning, and it took me a half hour to find them. I laughed my butt off when I realized what she had done.

Copper learned a new trick, since Cricket wasn't here. She would walk or sit behind us and sneeze to be picked up. It was hilarious. Now mind you, we were already picking her up 24/7, but apparently she was trying to make up for 10 years of not being able to be picked up in front of Cricket. It was actually bittersweet most days; we finally got to do a lot more with Copper without Cricket, due to Cricket's feisty personality.

We loved to watch Copper sleep. She would roll over on her back with all fours in the air and put her front paws together and clean them with her eyes closed, resembling a prayer position, and then fall asleep.

She would take walks, no, I mean runs, with the kids in the circle driveway, and she had a blast with no leash. She eventually fell right into Cricket's duties; it was strange but funny. She would sit on the back of the couch and alert us if there was a cat in the garden or a visitor.

She even greeted, in record-breaking time, the mail lady who wasn't impressed. Now, it was a different dog scaring her. I reassured her that my fluff ball meant no harm.

When we sat down at night to watch television, she would sit with us for awhile but then move over to the opposite end of the couch, where Cricket used to go to sleep. Unless it was a scary movie on, she would come back to sit with us. I would lift her up every night, though, when I went to bed and put her in her own bed and gave her kisses.

Another new trick she learned, to my and my husband's surprise was in the truck she started showing her teeth (what teeth she had) and growling. We finally figured out that there were certain gas stations Swanny would stop to get her a treat, and if we went past those spots, she growled. It was hilarious when we figured it out. She would even growl to have the window rolled down! She was wasting no time for getting what she wanted. She also started barking her orders at the McDonald's drive-thru to the point where we had to start going in to get the food. We were amazed at her new found personality.

When Cricket died, I prayed really hard to God to give us some time with Copper. God gave us three days short of a year with her. After Cricket died, Copper got a lump, of all places, on her butt, which instantly made me take her to the vet's to get it checked. They tested it and it was only fat deposits. Wouldn't you know, that stupid thing in six months grew to the size of a golf ball and made her look like a boy! How embarrassing when people asked what his name was!

Then one day out of the blue, she started leaking pus and leaving marks on the furniture. I thought it was just a fluke. I waited two weeks before I finally took her to the vet -- no rushing this time. I wasn't ready to give her up. I knew it was pyometra. The vet said she looked healthy enough to try antibiotics, so I agreed to try.

Just prior to the vet's appointment, I reminded my husband of his promise, that it was his tough turn to put down our baby. It only took one more week until Copper was leaking blood and pus.

I knew it was time.

My husband kept saying, "Wait one more day," with tears in his eyes, but I had promised myself that after taking my half-dead pug to be put down, I wouldn't allow Copper to suffer, so I made the appointment.

We took several pictures this time of Copper and videotaped her running in the driveway with the kids. I didn't give her antibiotics that night and fed her pizza, which made us both smile. I played with her with

Squeakers and her other toys and took her for one last truck ride.

Then the next morning, I kissed her goodbye.

We had a hard time deciding what to bury her with, but finally decided on Squeakers and her favorite stuffed play dog. We kept her blanket. Most men do not cry, but take their dogs away and they bawl.

The days following were filled with tears and stomachaches. When a dog passes, much like when a human dies, each person will have certain memories that trigger tears of mourning. I put the doggie dishes away, along with the beds and blankets and toys. I enlarged an 8x10 happy picture of her and hung it in the kitchen. We couldn't sit and watch television for a couple nights because she wasn't there with us. We felt badly walking in the driveway, and when we came home from shopping, there was no happy wagging of the tails to greet us. There was no precious brown eyes watching us or belly rubs. Nobody cared if the mail lady showed up or if there was a cat in the garden. No more alerts to visitors, just silence. No more keeping the jingling of the keys quiet, or giving dog baths. No more fixing her breakfast. The silence some days was deafening. That unconditional love was gone, only to be carried in our hearts.

Some dog owners choose cremation, putting their dogs in urns to put on their nightstand. Some choose to decorate their houses with photos. Others do elaborate burial plots in their backyards. Then there are some who choose to get another pet to fill that void in their life.

So you ask me what I am doing to survive this sad time. I am writing this book of memories because I don't want to forget. I want to remember so I can heal.

I'm delighted to know that God chose Swanny and I to be our two dogs' guardian humans.

CHAPTER 17

Heaven for Dogs

Upon surfing the Internet, I noticed that many people have written books on their beliefs of pets going to heaven. I did not write this part of the story to give you false hope but to give you reassurance that your pets are being watched over. This chapter was inspired from a two-year-old boy who God used to convince us that our dogs are in heaven.

I am going to recall the details of this day exactly how they happened, fully realizing that everyone has their own beliefs. To those of you who believe already, this will be of no surprise, but to those who don't, may I bring you hope -- the kind of hope that heals broken hearts.

I've mentioned before, throughout the book, that we babysit children of all ages. When Cricket passed, our hearts were sad and there was an emptiness in the house that only time would heal. We still had Copper, but she mourned the worst for Cricket. You could see the sadness in her eyes and her depressed actions every day because Cricket did not return. She did the best she could to fill Cricket's shoes to take her place.

We told the children the next day that Cricket had passed. Of course, there was some relief to the school-aged kids that their socks would not be attacked by Cricket when they got here after school. The other children asked where she was now, and we replied, "In heaven, playing with the angels." At the time, especially since we watched young children, we thought this response was the happiest way to say it, and it truly made me feel better. I think my original thoughts to myself were that the memories would eventually fade.

I always knew there would be animals in heaven, like the lions and sheep that the Bible says are lying together and getting along. I also thought pets here on earth were just temporary for our enjoyment. I will say now, though, the sorrow is not temporary at all -- it is very deep when losing a pet.

One of my two-year-olds was on vacation, so he hadn't been at the house when Cricket died, nor did he know that we buried her in the backyard. My husband decided to take a walk with the kids in the wooded picnic area around our house. Suddenly, the two-year-old pointed to the grave and said, "Cricket!"

My husband immediately got goose bumps and asked, "What did you say?"

Once again the little boy said, "Cricket," and pointed to the grave.

My husband, being alarmed said, "What is she doing?"

The little boy replied, "She's sitting there watching you."

I was in the house at the time and when I came outside, Swanny explained what happened. I was excited to hear this, due to my belief, which is that God uses little children to help adults who have stopped believing or never believed at all. I also believe that God uses simple people and children to baffle science at times.

I have to say, we joked about it when telling the child's mom, to not alarm her. I said to her, "Well, your little boy does not see dead people, but he does see dead animals!" She laughed it off, with no surprise, that he does have a good imagination. When I explained there was absolutely no way he could have known where she was buried, it seemed a little more eerie to her. I restated my beliefs, that God uses little children to help us adults.

It's funny though, Swanny over the years has had several family members pass on, and he has always wished to receive a sign from them, like others do at times. So when the little boy saw Cricket, he was having a hard time wrapping his head around the idea -- much like the story of doubting Thomas in the Bible.

Like I mentioned earlier, after Cricket passed, I asked God to give us some time with Copper, and he gave us three days short of a year of Cricket's death. Now three, the same little boy was on vacation during Copper's death, so he heard the sad news from his mom. Two weeks had gone by after her death, and the boy returned on a 70 degree day. We got the kids ready to go outside, with me lagging behind as usual. My husband walked them out to the playground, and the little boy said, "There Copper is!"

My husband, stunned, asked, "Where?"

"Over there, in the yard, watching you."

Swanny wanted to know more so he then questioned, "Is that all you see?"

"I see Cricket sitting next to her." Instant tears came to my husband's eyes. As I caught up to them, my husband said crying, "If I had any doubts before, I don't now," and explained the miraculous event that happened.

I no longer have tears of sadness; I actually have tears of joy all the time. Are Copper and Cricket wagging their tails like crazy in sheer happiness now? Are they splashing through rain puddles, or is Copper maybe learning how to swim? She sure did love her baths. Maybe Cricket is having races with bunny rabbits, because surely they are both fast. I could see Cricket and Copper hanging out with children in heaven, which would remind them of their first home, here on earth. I do wonder, though, if Cricket now tolerates the birds talking and singing without having a heart attack! I hope that Cricket has made friends, and I think Copper will make sure of it.

It's so funny to think they were both sitting a world away, Copper on the couch and Cricket in heaven waiting for each other. It reminds me of older couples, that when one passes on, the other one passes soon after that to be reunited. I could hear Swanny and I saying, "No, you go first! No, you!" Ironically, now we are saying in laughter, I want to go first to see the puppies!

Copper must have been so surprised to see Cricket again. I can just imagine Cricket waiting for her, so they could explore heaven together! I'm sure they are both having fun but still on the lookout for me and Swanny.

When a two-year-old sees something outrageous once, adults sometimes have a hard time believing it. When that same child, now three, sees something again with such perfect timing, how can you not believe? The God I love, would not show us through a child's eyes that my dogs were safe and alive unless it was true. I am beyond excited to see them, and may everyone that believes in Jesus, as told in the Bible, have the same joy of seeing their beloved pets again too.

Just when you think the story has ended, here come the tears again; that's just how love works. As I wonder to myself when I walk by their graves: Did I play with them enough? Did I pet them enough, and were their beds comfortable? Did they really like the food I fed them, as I tried to maintain their weight? How many times did their water dishes run dry and I felt badly? Should I have run them outside in the rain, just for the fun of it? Would they have enjoyed a movie about dogs once in awhile, or maybe even taken to a dog park to make new friends? I will never know.

I do know, though, that there will be no more sorrow when I get to heaven. So when I do see my dogs, I know that all my mortal mistakes and insufficiencies will be forgiven.

CHAPTER 18

One More Sighting

I would consider myself remiss, if I didn't add this one last chapter. Earlier on, I had the thought pass through my head of why my husband got to partake in the first two sightings and not me. I dismissed the thought, as our pets needed to reassure him more.

I worked around their grave sight, from time to time, cleaning up and planting flowers, and I would say hello to them, in case they could hear me. Swanny had even mentioned putting a pretty fence around their graves. I quickly said no, thinking that if they do return, I didn't want them thinking we were fencing them in.

Just when I thought God was done surprising me, he surprised me again.

We had a beautiful spring day three weeks after the passing of Copper, so I took the kids out to play. Swanny did not feel well and stayed inside that day. After about 20 minutes on the playground, a ball rolled off into the grass. Another three-year-old boy (not the first one mentioned in the story) went to fetch the ball. Then, as fast as a bullet, the boy came running back to the playground yelling, "Get back, two dogs! Get back!" I asked the boy if the two dogs were Cricket and Copper, even though I already knew it was, and he said, laughing nervously, "Yes!"

Now, wouldn't you know, that when this happened the two-year-old girl I was watching, who had only seen Copper once before she passed, said excitedly, "Where, where, where is Copper?" I replied again that she was in heaven playing with the angels. That little girl stood on the edge of the playground yelling for Copper for five minutes. When I asked her what she was doing, she replied, "I need to find Copper, so I can pick her up and give her to you, so you won't be sad anymore." I was speechless.

I have to say one more time, if you believe in Jesus like the Bible says, you will see your pets again! Jesus not only gives eternal life to your pets as a gift, he also offers the gift of eternal life to us, if we accept it.

Your pets miss you dearly and are waiting for you!

End

About the Author

Trini Deyarmin, a licensed in-home daycare provider, lives in Medina, NY with her husband. She has two grown boys and has been caring for other children for twenty-seven years. In her spare time she loves to be in her flower garden or to make primitive crafts to sell.